STUDY GUIDE

PURE FLIX PRESENTS

DO YOU
BELIEVE?

A STUDY TO HELP YOU PUT YOUR FAITH INTO ACTION

OUTRE/CH®

Do You Believe? *Study Guide*
© 2015 by Outreach, Inc.
© 2015 Pure Flix Entertainment, LLC
Photographs used by permission of Pure Flix Entertainment, LLC.

Published by Outreach, Inc., Colorado Springs, CO 80919.
www.Outreach.com

All Scripture quotations are taken from THE HOLY BIBLE, NEW INTERNA-TIONAL VERSION®, NIV® Copyright © 1973, 1978, 1984, 2011 by Biblica, Inc.® Used by permission. All rights reserved worldwide.

ISBN: 9781942027157
Written by Katie and Darren Sutton
Cover Design by Tim Downs
Interior Design by Alexia Garaventa
Edited by Tia Smith
Printed in the United States of America

TABLE OF CONTENTS

FOREWORD

Hey, what's up? Michael from the Newsboys.

The way I see it, theaters are like little mini-concerts nationwide. And in 2014, the Newsboys had the opportunity to play to millions across America thanks to the movie *God's Not Dead*. What an awesome experience! And the best part about it is that the Gospel got to be shared through a medium that is usually the "Hollywood machine."

This year we got to do it all over again! The Newsboys were blessed to be part of the follow-up film to *God's Not Dead*. If you agree that God is alive and roaring like a lion, then *Do You Believe?* will dare you to live like it!

Let's be honest, this world is a dark place. We're inundated with stories of death, violence, and trouble. But keep in mind that the darker it gets, the more the light shines through. What our world needs right now is Christians who will live their faith and share the name of Jesus wherever they go. That's why I'm glad you're holding this study guide. As you go through it, you'll find Scriptures, insights, and ideas to share the Gospel with friends who desperately need to hear it.

God may not ask you to speak to millions of people. You may not be called to perform on a stage. But remember this: Your role is every bit as important—maybe even more so—because God is asking you to shine His light into your world. Will you? Do you believe?

I dare you to live it!

Michael Tait
Lead Singer of the Newsboys

INTRODUCTION

Do you believe? Truly believe? Because true belief requires doing something. Faith without action is no faith at all.

James 2:26 is a challenge! *"As the body without the spirit is dead, so faith without deeds is dead."*

As you remember characters and stories from the film *Do You Believe?*, you'll be pushed to take the cross from your "proverbial pocket" and wear it smack on your sleeve. You'll begin to look beyond circumstances and start seeing defining moments. Your eyes will no longer focus on the here and now, but rather you'll see deeply into the heart of Jesus as you're compelled to give feet to your faith.

Perhaps you'll embark on this journey personally. As you spend time in the Word and reflecting on Scripture, you'll identify with characters in the film and begin to wonder what you might do in a similar circumstance. Soon, you'll be looking at every circumstance as a God-ordained moment in time that requires a choice from you—a choice to act on God's prompting or ignore it for another day, a choice to meet the needs of someone in your sphere of influence or allow them to silently suffer, a choice to embrace every single moment in time as a chance to live tangibly what you believe in your heart.

Or maybe you'll choose to share this study with friends. Together you'll explore what it means to prove your faith by doing. Maybe you'll confess to one another regrets over opportunities that passed with inaction. You could begin to embrace the fellowship of the accountable, bringing to life Proverbs 27:17, sharpening one another "as iron sharpens iron." Or you'll simply choose to embrace hope and perseverance as you fling Jesus into every moment—making faith in action the hallmark of your camaraderie.

Studying on your own or in a group . . . your life will change forever. Because face it, each of us meets Jesus only because someone else had the courage to act on what they believed. And you could be that person in the life of someone who desperately needs the hope only Christ provides.

No matter how large or small, it's a monumental moment—integrating opportunities to serve and do and risk into a life of faith. But Jesus commanded us to be doers, not simply believers or hearers. So when this study is concluded, the quiet question will remain: "If you believe, then what are you gonna do about it?"

This study will help you answer that question.

HOW TO USE THIS STUDY

Springboarding from the PureFlix movie *Do You Believe?*, these four lessons are multifaceted. They are intended to be used as a four-week study series. However, they are written individually enough that you can seize spiritual truth and challenge from any lesson on its own.

While these lessons can be used solely by virtue of viewing the specific video clips (or even reading the scene descriptions), they were written with the entire movie *Do You Believe?* in mind. To garner the most discussion and inspire the most thorough self-examination, the best way to use this study is to view the movie in its entirety, then use the clips as reference reminders.

The **Discuss** section is structured to be hands-on, conversational dialogue with a small group. The questions are devised to foster conversation with one another. They are easily adapted for a teacher/student setting but work best in the context of a small group.

The **Explore** section is designed with the individual participant in mind. While the questions can be utilized in a small group context, they're truly structured to help you become more contemplative and introspective. Space is provided for journaling responses to the answers.

The **Respond** section will challenge you, both corporately and solely, to take a moment for personal reflection. It provides practical application and closes out the lesson with a tangible reminder of what you've thought about during the study.

Finally, the **Persist** section provides additional study passages for future, individual study. Think of this section as devotional ideas that you can use during the week to continue thinking about the truths you're learning within the study.

The most important thing to remember is that each lesson is designed to be thought provoking regardless of your faith stage. It's useful to pre-believers, folks with newfound faith, or Christ followers who have been pursuing Jesus for years. Keep in mind, the broadest discussion will be found in a group that utilizes folks in various stages of faith development.

WEEK 1:

DO YOU BELIEVE GOD HAS A PLAN?

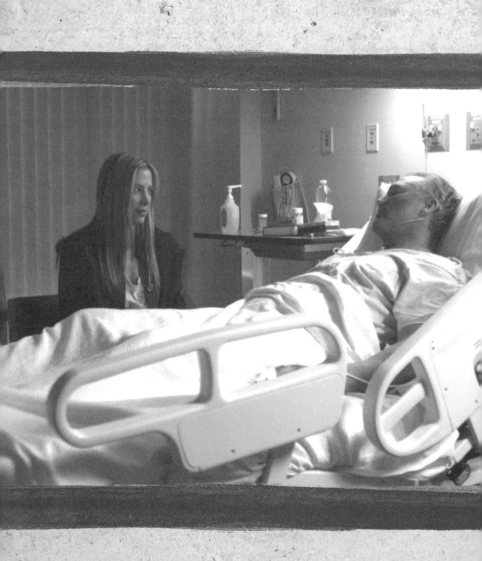

KEY SCRIPTURE

"Praise be to the God and Father of our Lord Jesus Christ, who has blessed us in the heavenly realms with every spiritual blessing in Christ. For he chose us in him before the creation of the world to be holy and blameless in his sight. In love he predestined us for adoption to sonship through Jesus Christ, in accordance with his pleasure and will—to the praise of his glorious grace, which he has freely given us in the One he loves." —Ephesians 1:3-6

CENTRAL TRUTH

Our lives may be complicated with the struggle of sin, but God has always had a plan to save us.

KEY MOVIE SCENE

Watch Clip 1.

Joe is in the hospital dying. Samantha comes to see him. He is a strong Christian who knows what it means to have been forgiven for a wasted life. He understands that all of the mistakes he made eventually led him to Jesus. He wants Samantha to know that God loves her even though life is hard.

DISCUSS

- What are some common ways people react to hard times?

- Think about someone you know who amazed you with the way they handled a difficult situation. What about them impressed you the most?

- How could tough times change the way someone lives out their future?

- What one word sums up what you would like for people to say about you at the end of your life?

Life is a journey loaded with ups and downs, sometimes all at the same time. But what if every moment of our lives is leading us to some grand finale more spectacular than any scene on Broadway? What if the choices we make and the consequences we endure could open our eyes to something so much bigger than our imaginations could conjure—with every moment full of purpose and every experience leading us toward the one thing we could truly connect to in life? It's hard to accept that our pain could be exactly what leads us to peace and hope. But what if that was always the plan? What if God has always had a plan to save us from the inevitably hollow end of a life lived in hopelessness and sin? Could He be using those awful struggles to point us toward the deliverance we seek? Do you believe God has a plan?

EXPLORE

1. SIN AND STRUGGLE ARE OUR REALITY.
Read Romans 3:23-24. *"For all have sinned and fall short of the glory of God, and all are justified freely by his grace through the redemption that came by Christ Jesus."*

Read Colossians 1:13-14. *"For he has rescued us from the dominion of darkness and brought us into the kingdom of the Son he loves, in whom we have redemption, the forgiveness of sins."*

- How do you define sin in your life?

- What struggles are you currently facing?

- What does the Bible say is God's role in our sin and struggle?

- Do you give God the freedom to exercise that role in your life? Why or why not? If so, what does that look like?

Sin is a part of life that is hard to avoid. We are born into a sinful world with the natural inclination to go our own way instead of submitting to God's way. All of us are headed on a path that leads to destruction. Without intervention, everyone's life would end hopeless and helpless.

If you are a Christ follower, consider your life before you embraced Jesus. Perhaps you share a similar story with Joe . . . a life of regrets. Maybe your life was laced with decisions that drove you to a defining moment with Christ. Or maybe your testimony feels a little more "tame"—you followed Jesus before your life spiraled too far off course. In both cases, the end is the same. We are separated from a life-giving relationship with God, hopeless to connect with Him on our own without the intervention and intercession of Christ.

Maybe you're still exploring the claims of Christ, discerning whether or not this "Jesus thing" is for you. The amazing truth found in the Bible—and in the lives of people around you—is that Jesus is ready and waiting with redemption, forgiveness, compassion, and love for us. His embrace is not contingent on where we find ourselves in the story—hard choices, easy lives, difficult consequences, solid faith, or doubting minds. He waits with compassion and forgiveness to rescue no matter where we are in our faith journey.

2. OUR SALVATION HAS BEEN SECURED IN JESUS.
Read John 3:16-17. *"For God so loved the world that he gave his one and only Son, that whoever believes in him shall not perish but have eternal life. For God did not send his Son into the world to condemn the world, but to save the world through him."*

God's plan is that all people might be saved through Jesus. He doesn't want anyone to be eternally condemned.

- What was Jesus's primary purpose in the world?

- When you think about your own life, do you live like you are condemned by your choices or like you have been saved from them?

- What can you do to ensure that you live a life free from the guilt of regret?

God made a way for us to be rescued from the pitfalls of this world. So why is it that most of us still live like we are condemned? It's easy to stay chained to bad decisions and lasting consequences. But that was never God's intent. He wants us to live free from the bondage of our past mistakes. To do anything less cheapens His sacrifice—as though His crucifixion was enough to get us a ticket into heaven, but not quite sufficient to handle our baggage claim.

When Jesus willfully became the bridge between us and God, He bridged the entire gap—start to finish, past to future. When we maintain regrets, we take our future out of the hands of God and white-knuckle that self-condemnation. We hold on to what chains us to our past. It was never God's intention for the past to define us.

Read 2 Corinthians 5:17. *"Therefore, if anyone is in Christ, the new creation has come: The old has gone, the new is here!"*

Read John 10:10. *"The thief comes only to steal and kill and destroy; I have come that they may have life, and have it to the full."*

3. FORGIVENESS IS OUR CHOICE.

God has made the offer of salvation available for anyone who will accept it. It's up to us to decide if we will allow Him to intervene. God's desire is that all of us would turn from sin and struggle and ask Him for help. He doesn't want even one of us to collapse under the weight of this world, but the decision is ultimately up to us. God intervenes when He is asked.

Read Acts 2:36-39. *"'Therefore let all Israel be assured of this: God has made this Jesus, whom you crucified, both Lord and Messiah.' When the people heard this, they were cut to the heart and said to Peter and the other apostles, 'Brothers, what shall we do?' Peter replied, 'Repent and be baptized, every one of you, in the name of Jesus Christ for the forgiveness of your sins. And you will receive the gift of the Holy Spirit. The promise is for you and your children and for all who are far off—for all whom the Lord our God will call.'"*

- What do you think prevents people from accepting God's forgiveness?

- When you think about your life, can you remember a time when you asked Jesus to forgive you? If not, what is stopping you from asking right now?

4. GOD HAS ALWAYS HAD A PLAN FOR US.

There has never been a moment in time that God was not thinking about you. His plan has always been to rescue you from sin. He has always wanted a relationship with you. He never wanted you to be distressed without Him. He has always loved you. He has always been "for" you.

Read Ephesians 1:3-6. *"Praise be to the God and Father of our Lord Jesus Christ, who has blessed us in the heavenly realms with every spiritual blessing in Christ. For he chose us in him before the creation of the world to be holy and blameless in his sight. In love he predestined us for adoption to sonship through Jesus Christ, in accordance with his pleasure and will—to the praise of his glorious grace, which he has freely given us in the One he loves."*

Jesus proved His love with action before you were ever born. He knew what it meant to sacrifice everything for you, and He was willing to do what God had asked of Him for your sake. He willingly died for your sin so that you would have the opportunity to know God.

Consider a family expecting a new baby. Maybe you're thinking of your first child—or another family member's journey. Remember the excitement? The anticipation? The joy? Bags were packed for the hospital. The nursery was pristine, perfect in every way.

The mobile was hung at the perfect height over the crib. The baby's room may have been the only room in the house to have a fresh coat of paint since move-in day. The anticipation was almost overwhelming to the parents-to-be. *And the baby wasn't even here yet!* Jesus's sacrifice was His preparation for a relationship with you just like new parents prepare the room for their newborn. That's how it is with Jesus as He waits for us to "ready ourselves" for Him. He's anticipating our relationship. He's dreaming over our future. He's planning, preparing, hoping, loving. And He's repeating your name over and over again as He waits.

Read John 17:1-4. *"After Jesus said this, he looked toward heaven and prayed: 'Father, the hour has come. Glorify your Son, that your Son may glorify you. For you granted him authority over all people that he might give eternal life to all those you have given him. Now this is eternal life: that they know you, the only true God, and Jesus Christ, whom you have sent. I have brought you glory on earth by finishing the work you gave me to do.'"*

- What evidence do you have that God has always had a plan for you?

- How does it make you feel to know that Jesus planned to sacrifice for you before the world was created?

- What benefits do those who know Jesus experience in God's plan?

God planned to give us everything He would give to His own Son before we even knew Him or accepted His salvation. He made a way for us to know Him despite seemingly impossible circumstances. Jesus willingly submitted His life for our salvation, and this was all planned before the foundation of the earth was laid.

Read Romans 5:8. *"But God demonstrates his own love for us in this: While we were still sinners, Christ died for us."*

- How does the knowledge of God's plan change the way you live your life?

- How can living like God had a plan affect those around you?

Though sin and its consequences have blighted our world, we can see that God has always had a plan to save us from its despair. Long before the first human turned away from God, Jesus planned to sacrifice Himself to save us from our regrets. Forgiveness is available, and it has been offered to us. God uses every moment of our lives to signal to us that He is here and that He wants us to be eternally adopted as His children. The most joyful of times to the most difficult of times all point toward God's plan to save us. It's up to us how we will respond to His amazing plan.

- How would you explain to a friend what you have learned about God's plan?

Respond

- Take a moment to think about the most difficult and most joyful times in your life. Write a couple of them down on the left side of a piece of paper. Now, pray that God will show you where He was in the midst of that time. Sit in silence for a few moments and see what He reveals to you. Write that down on the right side of your paper. After you have waited in quiet for God to speak, fold your paper and tuck it into your Bible study material. Over the next weeks, if God reveals anything new to you about His intervention in your journey, add it to your paper.

- Go to the closest window and look outside. As you view the scenery, consider that before all of this was created, God had your life in mind. Thank Him for providing you with a way out of sin and giving you a future of privilege as His adopted child in heaven.

- Make a list of things you are willing to turn away from to pursue a life of following Jesus. Post your list in a place where you will see it every day. Pray and ask God to begin the work of changing you into who He wants you to be. Ask Him to guide your steps as you begin a new life in Him or recommit to following in His way.

PERSIST

Read Acts 2:22-24. *"Fellow Israelites, listen to this: Jesus of Nazareth was a man accredited by God to you by miracles, wonders and signs, which God did among you through him, as you yourselves know. This man was handed over to you by God's deliberate plan and foreknowledge; and you, with the help of wicked men, put him to death by nailing him to the cross. But God raised him from the dead, freeing him from the agony of death, because it was impossible for death to keep its hold on him."*

God had a deliberate plan for Jesus's life and death. He was in control the entire time. How amazing to believe that He has seen and planned out our lives as well! Are we fighting against that plan or submitting to it as Jesus did?

Read Ephesians 1:3-14. *"Praise be to the God and Father of our Lord Jesus Christ, who has blessed us in the heavenly realms with every spiritual blessing in Christ. For he chose us in him before the creation of the world to be holy and blameless in his sight. In love he predestined us for adoption to sonship through Jesus Christ, in accordance with his pleasure and will—to the praise of his glorious grace, which he has freely given us in the One he loves. In him we have redemption through his blood, the forgiveness of sins, in accordance with the riches of God's grace that he lavished on us. With all wisdom and understanding, he made known to us the mystery of his will according to his good pleasure, which he purposed in Christ, to be put into effect when the times reach their fulfillment—to bring unity to all things in heaven and on earth under Christ. In him we were also chosen, having been predestined according to the plan of him who works out everything in conformity with the purpose of his will, in order that we, who were the first to put our hope in Christ, might be for the praise of his glory. And you also were included in Christ when you heard the message of truth, the gospel of your salvation. When you believed, you were marked in him with a seal, the promised Holy Spirit, who is a deposit guaranteeing our inheritance until the redemption of those who are God's possession—to the praise of his glory."*

God has an elaborate, time-sensitive plan for us in Christ Jesus that was laid out even before He created the world. His plan works out according to His will, and we were always included in it.

Read Jeremiah 29:11-13. *"For I know the plans I have for you,' declares the LORD, 'plans to prosper you and not to harm you, plans to give you hope and a future. Then you will call on me and come and pray to me, and I will listen to you. You will seek me and find me when you seek me with all your heart.'"*

God has a plan for us to find Him. He wants us to have hope and a future.

WEEK 2:

DO YOU BELIEVE YOU ARE A PART OF GOD'S PLAN?

KEY SCRIPTURE

"And we know that in all things God works for the good of those who love him, who have been called according to his purpose. For those God foreknew he also predestined to be conformed to the image of his Son, that he might be the firstborn among many brothers and sisters. And those he predestined, he also called; those he called, he also justified; those he justified, he also glorified." —Romans 8:28-30

CENTRAL TRUTH

Every individual is a part of God's plan. It's our choice to recognize God's work in the world or to deny His involvement in the experiences we have every day. We can choose to be willing, wholehearted participants in God's plan or we can resist it and miss all that He has purposed for our lives.

KEY MOVIE SCENE

Watch Clip 2.

Dr. Farell is having dinner with his girlfriend, Andrea, when he sees a couple praying over their meal. The doctor becomes offended at the overture and mocks how people give thanks to God for what happens in their lives. He feels the chef made the food, doctors save people's lives, and the thanks should go to the ones who actually do the work—not to a so-called God who doesn't even show up to do His own work.

DISCUSS

- Do you think Dr. Farell has a valid point? Explain.

- What can people accomplish without God?

- When do you think it is appropriate to claim accomplishments as our own doing rather than as God's handiwork?

- How can God use people who don't know Him or respect Him to further His plan?

- What are some ways people might take credit for God's work without realizing it?

Consider for a moment that this may be the way we treat God's actions in our lives. Although we might not say it overtly like Dr. Farell did, do our actions express a disbelief that God is really in control? Do we take credit where God should have the glory?

Read James 1:16-17. *"Don't be deceived, my dear brothers and sisters. Every good and perfect gift is from above, coming down from the Father of the heavenly lights, who does not change like shifting shadows."*

When God created the universe and set the stars in motion, He already had a plan not only for the salvation of humanity but for each individual who would ever live in the course of history. If we believe that God has a plan, we should acknowledge that His plan is still in progress. He is working even now to further His intention to save all who would accept His forgiveness. His desire is that we would participate in His plan of salvation for the world. Participation requires us to recognize that God is currently at work in people's lives all around us.

EXPLORE

1. GOD IS AT WORK IN PEOPLE'S LIVES ALL AROUND US.

Read Romans 1:20. *"For since the creation of the world God's invisible qualities—his eternal power and divine nature—have been clearly seen, being understood from what has been made, so that people are without excuse."*

Read Ecclesiastes 3:11. *"He has made everything beautiful in its time. He has also set eternity in the human heart; yet no one can fathom what God has done from beginning to end."*

- What are some clues God has given us that He has a plan for our world?

- What does the work of man look like in our world compared to the work of God?

Have you ever been enthralled by a specific piece of artwork or architecture? Maybe you have visited an art gallery with some amazing paintings or divine sculptures. Or maybe there is a home or business in your town that you look at every single time you pass it. Have you met the artist, the architect, the builder, or the craftsman? Chances are you have admired their beautiful creation, all while appreciating their "invisible qualities." (For example: "Wow! That must have taken forever." Or, "Look at the detail in that home! Everything is custom.")

The truth is, unless you have met the creator, you don't actually know firsthand any of the assumptions you've made by looking at their handiwork. It's simply evident through the design.

God's plans for each of us are much like that—invisible to the naked eye but obviously intentional when we pay attention.

Read Romans 8:28-30. *"And we know that in all things God works for the good of those who love him, who have been called according to his purpose. For those God foreknew he also predestined to be conformed to the image of his Son, that he might be the firstborn among many brothers and sisters. And those he predestined, he also called; those he called, he also justified; those he justified, he also glorified."*

- What does it mean to be "called according to his purpose"?

- How is God at work in the life of every believer?

- How can you recognize when God is at work around you?

Do you remember a time when God was working a purpose, even though you may not have sensed it at the time? Have you ever shared that story? Much like the example on page 27, when we find an exquisite art piece or an enthralling building, we almost always tell someone about it. ("Have you ever seen that old Victorian house on Central Street? It's stunning . . . especially during the holidays!")

God's purposeful working in your life is a beautiful art piece, sometimes invisible to the naked eye. Share that story with someone. Priceless works of art are meant to be shared—and the story of God's work in your life is truly unique and priceless.

Read Genesis 45:4-8. *"Then Joseph said to his brothers, 'Come close to me.' When they had done so, he said, 'I am your brother Joseph, the one you sold into Egypt! And now, do not be distressed and do not be angry with yourselves for selling me here, because it was to save lives that God sent me ahead of you. For two years now there has been famine in the land, and for the next five years there will be no plowing and reaping. But God sent me ahead of you to preserve for you a remnant on earth and to save your lives by a great deliverance. So then, it was not you who sent me here, but God. He made me father to Pharaoh, lord of his entire household and ruler of all Egypt.'"*

2. GOD WANTS US TO RECOGNIZE OUR PLACE IN HIS PLAN.

Joseph was the second youngest of twelve brothers. God had given him many gifts and talents. Joseph had been told by God that he would one day serve Him as a ruler. While he waited for God's promise to come true, Joseph used his talents in arrogance and goaded his brothers by flaunting the special favor shown to him. One day, they became fed up and decided to sell Joseph into slavery (Genesis 37).

For many years, Joseph was a slave in Egypt. Throughout that time, God continued to use Joseph and develop his gifts. When the time was right in God's plan, against all odds and contrary to his obvious circumstances, Joseph was given an audience with Pharaoh, the ruler of Egypt. Joseph humbly used his gifts to speak to Pharaoh, who showed him favor and appointed him ruler over all Egypt, second only to Pharaoh himself, in a position that exactly used all the talents that Joseph had developed while he was in slavery.

Joseph understood his place in God's plan. Even though he had suffered greatly because of his brothers' actions, he saw how God had worked all things together for his good and for the sake of many others.

Read Genesis 50:20. *"You intended to harm me, but God intended it for good to accomplish what is now being done, the saving of many lives."*

- What could have happened if Joseph had not recognized that God had a bigger plan for the course of his life?

- How can someone still be participating in God's plan when they are seemingly not experiencing victory in their circumstances?

In the movie clip we discussed, Dr. Farell saw only one small part of what was happening in the world around him. He couldn't see that there may have been something bigger than himself at work. In the masterpiece that God was painting, the doctor saw the brushstrokes of the painting but failed to see the landscape that was developing on the entire canvas. Joseph may have had times when he saw only the brushstrokes in his circumstances, but he was faithful to trust God that everything would come together for his good. Joseph continued to serve the Lord even when he could not understand God's whole plan.

- What do you think is missed when people don't consider their role in God's plan?

- How can we develop a lifestyle of looking for God in our circumstances, good or bad?

- Have you ever doubted your role in what God was doing?

3. GOD WANTS TO USE OUR GIFTS, SKILLS, AND EXPERIENCES IN THE COURSE OF HIS PLAN.

When we recognize that God wants us to play a role in the lives of others who may come to know Him, we might wonder what we have to offer Him.

Read 1 Timothy 4:14-15. *"Do not neglect your gift, which was given you through prophecy when the body of elders laid their hands on you. Be diligent in these matters; give yourself wholly to them, so that everyone may see your progress."*

- How has God used someone you know to work good in the lives of others? What would you say is that person's primary gift, talent, or skill?

- How is God using you in His plan, and why are your skills important?

Because we're human, we see in the immediate—what is happening right this moment and how it impacts the present. But God paints on a much wider canvas. Many times we can't even see the edges of the landscape He is constructing. Sometimes, all we see is a blank canvas. That's why it's so important, when looking at our current circumstance, to consider the filter of our unique qualities and attributes. We may not understand why we are currently without a job or facing relational difficulties, but our uniqueness—our ability to weather the storm, our capacity to trust in moments when we want to walk away, our resolution to stand squarely in

God's will regardless of circumstance—may communicate God's story to someone watching this artwork unfold.

It's almost like looking at the painter's palette rather than at the painting. The palette of paint swatches contains the qualities that prepare us for use; the mixing tray will ultimately transform the blank canvas into something beautiful. The canvas remains flat and unremarkable until what's in the hand of the artist becomes readied and applied to the scene. You and all the things that make you "you" form the palette God uses to revolutionize ordinary into extraordinary.

Read 2 Corinthians 1:3-4. *"Praise be to the God and Father of our Lord Jesus Christ, the Father of compassion and the God of all comfort, who comforts us in all our troubles, so that we can comfort those in any trouble with the comfort we ourselves receive from God."*

- Why would God want to use our pain in the lives of those around us?

- Can you recount a time when someone else's experience impacted your own story? Have you ever shared that with the person whose life you were watching? Should you?

- How can we surrender our good and bad experiences to be used for God's glory?

- What experiences in your life do you see God using in someone else's life?

4. GOD INVITES US TO BE USED.

Read 1 Samuel 3:7-10. *"Now Samuel did not yet know the LORD: The word of the LORD had not yet been revealed to him.*

"A third time the LORD called, 'Samuel!' And Samuel got up and went to Eli and said, 'Here I am; you called me.'

"Then Eli realized that the LORD was calling the boy. So Eli told Samuel, 'Go and lie down, and if he calls you, say, "Speak, LORD, for your servant is listening."' So Samuel went and lay down in his place.

"The LORD came and stood there, calling as at the other times, 'Samuel! Samuel!'

"Then Samuel said, 'Speak, for your servant is listening.'"

When Samuel was young, God began speaking to him about how he would be used. Even before Samuel recognized the voice of God or knew Him personally, God called out to Samuel to get his attention.

- What are some key points that can be gleaned from Samuel's experience of learning to listen to God?

- In your own life, how do you recognize when God is speaking to you?

- Have there been times in your life when God was trying to get your attention but you ignored or misunderstood His voice? Are you listening now? What is He saying?

- If God has the ability to do anything or everything without us, then why does He choose to use us?

- How do we identify where God wants us to act in His plan? In our own life? In others' circumstances? Globally?

God is actively at work in the lives of the people around us. He wants us to open our eyes and look for ways He can use us in His plan to reach others. He will use all that we have, all that we are, and all that we have been through as a part of His overall plan. Every day He extends an invitation for us to be active participants in what He is doing in the world. When God calls out, will you deny that you are hearing His voice? Will you attribute the stirring in your heart to something other than the prompting of God in your life? Or will you submit to Him, asking for a clear and obvious way to accomplish your role in His plan?

Respond

- Throughout this lesson, how has God revealed to you that you are being called into His purpose? In the next few moments, begin your first act of responding to God's invitation to be a part of His work. Do something practical to obey His prompting. Pray out loud and say, "Speak, Lord, for Your servant is listening." If God has put someone on your mind, call them, write a letter of encouragement, visit them, but act immediately once you know what to do. Don't let God's prompting slip by this time.

- On a separate sheet of paper, list as many of your talents, gifts, and skills as you can think of in five minutes. Now put a check mark beside the ones that you know God has used to further His plan. Circle the remaining items on your list. Ask God how He wants to use these gifts and skills in His plan in the future. Write down any answers He immediately gives to you. Commit to using all that you have to offer for God's glory.

- Think about a time when you moved forward with a decision without asking God for His plan.

    – How did your plan work out for you?

    – Who was affected by your plan?

    – How might your actions have been different if you had considered God's bigger plan for you?

– Do you have any pending plans that you need to commit to God?

• Pray that God will show you where He is at work and how He wants you to participate in His plan. Over the next week, memorize this verse: *"Commit your way to the LORD; trust in him and he will do this"* (Psalm 37:5).

PERSIST

The foremost atheists make no secret that they think anyone who believes in God is ignorant and uninformed. Have you ever wondered why some of the smartest intellectuals seem to reject Christianity?

Read 1 Corinthians 1:18-31. *"For the message of the cross is foolishness to those who are perishing, but to us who are being saved it is the power of God. For it is written: 'I will destroy the wisdom of the wise; the intelligence of the intelligent I will frustrate.' Where is the wise person? Where is the teacher of the law? Where is the philosopher of this age? Has not God made foolish the wisdom of the world? For since in the wisdom of God the world through its wisdom did not know him, God was pleased through the foolishness of what was preached to save those who believe. Jews demand signs and Greeks look for wisdom, but we preach Christ crucified: a stumbling block to Jews and foolishness to Gentiles, but to those whom God has called, both Jews and Greeks, Christ the power of God and the wisdom of God. For the foolishness of*

God is wiser than human wisdom, and the weakness of God is stronger than human strength.

"Brothers and sisters, think of what you were when you were called. Not many of you were wise by human standards; not many were influential; not many were of noble birth. But God chose the foolish things of the world to shame the wise; God chose the weak things of the world to shame the strong. God chose the lowly things of this world and the despised things—and the things that are not—to nullify the things that are, so that no one may boast before him. It is because of him that you are in Christ Jesus, who has become for us wisdom from God—that is, our righteousness, holiness and redemption. Therefore, as it is written: 'Let the one who boasts boast in the Lord.'"

Read Genesis 39–45 to see the whole story of Joseph and how God developed his gifts and skills through incredibly difficult circumstances in order to fulfill His ultimate plan.

WEEK 3:

DO YOU BELIEVE THAT FAITH REQUIRES ACTION?

Key Scripture

"Do not merely listen to the word, and so deceive yourselves. Do what it says." —James 1:22

Central Truth

Having faith in God requires belief followed by action. As Christians, we should not be content in the knowledge that God has a plan without having the desire to participate in it. The knowledge of Jesus's sacrifice for us should motivate us to act.

Key Movie Scene

Watch Clip 3.

Malachi, a seeming street person carrying a large wooden cross, approaches the vehicle of Pastor Matthew. Malachi talks with Matthew about believing in Jesus Christ. Matthew tells Malachi that he is a pastor. Then Malachi confronts Matthew with the demands of real belief in the cross. He asks, "If you believe, then the question is, what are you gonna do about it?" Matthew is shaken by the question.

Discuss

- What would your reaction have been to this interaction?

- What is the difference between belief and the demands of the cross?

- What about the story of Jesus and the cross motivates your faith?

- At what point does faith move from a "feeling" to a tangible "doing"?

Religious people rely on their faith to know that what they believe is true. But the message that Malachi emphasized to the pastor is that faith must be about more than belief. The fact that Jesus carried our cross and bore our punishment should motivate our actions. It doesn't just sprinkle our lives with good feelings and a future hope of heaven. It should soak us in thankfulness so drenching that we overflow with compassion for others. When we truly believe in what Jesus has done for us, we will feel compelled to intercede on the behalf of others. Only when we sacrifice for others can we understand what Jesus sacrificed for us. Our actions will prove the depth of our faith.

EXPLORE

1. GOD'S PLAN REQUIRES US TO HAVE FAITH.
Read Hebrews 11:1. *"Now faith is confidence in what we hope for and assurance about what we do not see."*

- What apprehensions do you have when you think about the act of faith?

- What do you think motivates people to believe in things that have not yet happened or that they cannot see?

- How does God prove His character when we act in faith? Why does faith seem counterintuitive to most of us?

Read Hebrews 11:6. *"And without faith it is impossible to please God, because anyone who comes to him must believe that he exists and that he rewards those who earnestly seek him."*

- How does this verse impact your view of faith?

- What rewards are available when we believe in Christ?

- What's the benefit of trusting God to use you in a plan you don't fully understand?

Faith will prompt us to do things that we know we can't do by ourselves. The action is bigger than something we could do on our own. Having confidence in God's plan when we cannot possibly see the outcome is the point at which we understand true faith. Faith knows that regardless of what happens, God will enact His plan when we are moved to action by His prompting.

2. FAITH IS MORE THAN BELIEF.

Read James 2:14-19. *"What good is it, my brothers and sisters, if someone claims to have faith but has no deeds? Can such faith save them? Suppose a brother or a sister is without clothes and daily food. If one of you says to them, 'Go in peace; keep warm and well fed,' but does nothing about their physical needs, what good is it? In the same way, faith by itself, if it is not accompanied by action, is dead.*

"But someone will say, 'You have faith; I have deeds.'

"Show me your faith without deeds, and I will show you my faith by my deeds. You believe that there is one God. Good! Even the demons believe that—and shudder."

Sometimes it's easy to mistake acts of commitment to Christian practices as acts of faith in God. Going to church, reading the Bible, praying, and preaching God's Word are all good, necessary, and commendable. But the Bible tells us that even the demons believe in God. They know Scripture and they know that God exists. They have seen Jesus and were participants in His death. They have a lot of knowledge of God's ways, but they lack one key factor that defines true faith: deeds.

Have you ever been to a restaurant that has a sample tray of desserts? When the server brings the tray to your table, you can see how delicious they look. But often what appear to be piles of whipped cream on decadent cake is not food at all. Not until you try to sneak a taste of those delectable desserts do you find out if you are getting a sweet bite of chocolate or a mouthful of wax. Just because something looks good on the outside doesn't mean that it's actually genuine. True faith goes beyond knowledge. True faith is tested by deeds.

Focus on James 2:18-19. *"But someone will say, 'You have faith; I have deeds.' Show me your faith without deeds, and I will show you my faith by my deeds. You believe that there is one God. Good! Even the demons believe that—and shudder."*

Read Romans 2:13. *"For it is not those who hear the law who are righteous in God's sight, but it is those who obey the law who will be declared righteous."*

- What are some ways that people mistake knowledge for faith?

- How much knowledge does it take to be saved?

- How can someone truly believe in God's plan if they never obey God's Word?

- What does acting in faith prove to us? What does it prove to God?

Anyone can say that they believe in Jesus, and anyone can study God's Word. True identification as a Christian means following Jesus's example of a godly life. Lots of people say they believe in Jesus, but their actions are contrary to the Bible. Salvation requires only our belief in Jesus as the Son of God sent to pay for our sins through His sacrifice on the cross. But the proof of our belief is the way we participate in God's plan for our lives. Jesus asks us to take up our own cross and daily follow Him. Our faith requires action.

3. FAITH REQUIRES ACTION.

Read Hebrews 13:16. *"And do not forget to do good and to share with others, for with such sacrifices God is pleased."*

Focus on James 2:15-17. *"Suppose a brother or a sister is without clothes and daily food. If one of you says to them, 'Go in peace; keep warm and well fed,' but does nothing about their physical needs, what good is it? In the same way, faith by itself, if it is not accompanied by action, is dead."*

- What prevents you from doing good? What compels you to do good?

- What are some ways that we can meet the physical needs as well as the spiritual needs of people around us?

At times, it seems like the Church has invested in a bright blinking sign that says, "Come in, you are welcome here!" Millions of dollars are spent making sure that Christians know how to be friendly and are open to interacting with people who don't know about Jesus when they come into our churches. We expect struggling people to be attracted by our flashy shows, relevant music, well-themed study series, and pretty lights—and sometimes we never take the actual step outside into the world to encounter those who really need our help. *These hopeless people may be standing in the parking lot terrified to come in while we stand inside terrified to go out.*

- Whose responsibility is it to take the first step in meeting needs?

- How would you meet the need of someone who has not asked for help?

- What apprehensions do Christians have about mingling with the secular world?

- How did Jesus handle those issues in His day?

Read Matthew 28:19-20. *"Therefore go and make disciples of all nations, baptizing them in the name of the Father and of the Son and of the Holy Spirit, and teaching them to obey everything I have commanded you. And surely I am with you always, to the very end of the age."*

In Jesus's last statement on this earth, He commanded His followers to "go." That's not a passive statement. It's an action step. And it's incredibly clear. God has provided opportunities all around us for us to act on our faith. We must develop eyes and hearts that recognize those opportunities. And then we need to muster the courage to obey. God always intended for us to participate in His plan to save a dying world. And while He might not *need* us to get the job done, He certainly *wants* us! Seizing opportunities to put faith into action usually has equitable consequences. God does something supernatural in the lives of those we're ministering to, but He also does a supernatural work within us. And the more we practice action faith, the more automatic and natural it becomes for us.

4. ACTIONS PROVE OUR TRUE BELIEF.
Read James 1:22. *"Do not merely listen to the word, and so deceive yourselves. Do what it says."*

Actions always speak louder than words. We all know stories of spouses who settle into a comfortable marriage and forget to demonstrate their love for the one they married. At some point, someone in the relationship usually exclaims, "I don't just need you to *tell* me you love me; I need you to *show* me." Action communicates loudly and in a more lasting way what our hearts and minds don't always reveal.

- Considering the analogy of the spousal relationship, what are your actions currently saying to Jesus? What do you want them to say?

- What are some places in your life where you may have become content to keep your Christianity to yourself?

- What does it look like to put actions to your faith?

- How does an active faith prove true belief to those around us?

If we believe that God has a plan for the world, then we must have faith to participate in His plan. Faith is so much more than a sedentary commitment to learning about God's Word. It's an active lifestyle of sacrifice that requires us to risk our comfort for the sake of others having the opportunity to know Christ. Action is a necessary part of our Christian walk because it proves our commitment to following in Jesus's way. A commitment to action is a commitment to sacrifice just as Jesus sacrificed for us.

RESPOND

- Think about someone you know who is experiencing challenges right now. Pray for them specifically. Now honestly answer the following questions.

    - How involved are you willing to become in this person's struggle?

    - Are you content to live out your Christian walk within the comfort of church services and Bible studies, or is God asking you to do more?

- What is He asking you to do?

- If acting in faith becomes messy, what are you willing to sacrifice to follow God's plan?

• When you are done, pray again and ask God to show you how you fit in His plan for this person. Ask Him to give you all you need to risk acting in faith. Then act!

• Read 1 Corinthians 3:18-19. *"Do not deceive yourselves. If any of you think you are wise by the standards of this age, you should become 'fools' so that you may become wise. For the wisdom of this world is foolishness in God's sight. As it is written: 'He catches the wise in their craftiness.'"*

- In what ways have you deceived yourself into believing that you are doing what is "best" rather than doing what God has prompted you to do?

– How does acting in faith seem foolish?

– How far are you willing to go to abandon an ordinary life of wisdom for a foolish life in Christ?

– What steps will you take today to start to become foolish for the sake of God's plan in your life?

PERSIST

Psalm 119 is a personal confession of obedience to acting on the things written in God's Word. The author transparently recounts his victories and struggles with following God's plan for his life. Spend some time meditating on this psalm. Choose a couple meaningful verses from the psalm to memorize. Hang these verses somewhere poignant and regularly visible to you.

Read Psalm 119:105-106. *"Your word is a lamp for my feet, a light on my path. I have taken an oath and confirmed it, that I will follow your righteous laws."*

WEEK 4:

DO YOU BELIEVE JESUS IS WORTH YOUR SACRIFICE?

KEY SCRIPTURE

"Then he said to them all: 'Whoever wants to be my disciple must deny themselves and take up their cross daily and follow me. For whoever wants to save their life will lose it, but whoever loses their life for me will save it. What good is it for someone to gain the whole world, and yet lose or forfeit their very self?'" —Luke 9:23-25

CENTRAL TRUTH

Submitting to God's plan requires sacrifice. Jesus asks us to give our whole lives to follow after Him.

KEY MOVIE SCENE

Watch Clip 4.

Bobby, an EMT, is sitting on a bench waiting to enter a courtroom. He is on his way to a disciplinary hearing that will determine if he loses his job and is sued for sharing his faith in Jesus with a dying man while he was on duty. Andrea, the lawyer who is suing him, sits down beside him and asks why he would choose to lose everything for the sake of "pushing your beliefs on others." Bobby says that if he is going to be deemed guilty of something, he would want it to be "the crime of being a Christian." Andrea is confused and seemingly untouched by his statement. She pulls a cross out of her pocket that Bobby had given to the dying man, and she ends the conversation with, "This cross is gonna cost you."

After the hearing, we see Bobby alone in the courtroom, and it is obvious that he has lost his job and the court case.

DISCUSS

- What does it mean to push your beliefs on other people?

- In your opinion, when is it appropriate to share your faith?

- What do you think of sharing your faith in the workplace?

- What kind of risk would you be taking to share your faith with a coworker? A neighbor? A relative? A stranger?

Bobby risked it all. He didn't accidentally lose his job or get caught in the crossfire of political correctness. He was given the opportunity to keep his job and avoid being sued if he recanted his actions with a simple promise never to do it again. The dying man had accepted Christ, and a rescindment from Bobby couldn't forfeit his place in eternity. But Bobby knew that God had a bigger plan for him. He was willing to sacrifice everything for the opportunity to tell even one more person about the forgiveness that Jesus has to offer.

Every day we have opportunities to share Jesus's salvation with people. With every opportunity comes sacrifice. Some of the sacrifices are small; others will cost us everything.

EXPLORE

1. ACTING IN GOD'S PLAN WILL REQUIRE SACRIFICE.

Read Romans 12:1. *"Therefore, I urge you, brothers and sisters, in view of God's mercy, to offer your bodies as a living sacrifice, holy and pleasing to God—this is your true and proper worship."*

- What do we offer to God when we sacrifice to be a part of His plan?

- What does it mean to become a living sacrifice?

- What kinds of things do people sacrifice for the cause of Christ?

While it may seem like God is asking a lot of us to sacrifice what we love for His plans, remember that He gave us forgiveness at the cost of His Son's life when we didn't deserve it. He then adopted us as His own children with the promise of rewards and the privilege of royalty after this world is gone. In perspective, it's only proper for us to sacrifice for His plans, and any sacrifice we make seems worth the cost!

2. JESUS SACRIFICED EVERYTHING FOR US.

Read 1 Peter 2:19-21. *"For it is commendable if someone bears up under the pain of unjust suffering because they are conscious of God. But how is it to your credit if you receive a beating for doing wrong and endure it? But if you suffer for doing good and you endure it, this is commendable before God. To this you were called, because Christ suffered for you, leaving you an example, that you should follow in his steps."*

- How does Jesus's example of sacrifice inspire us to sacrifice for the sake of others?

- Give some examples of people who sacrificed to participate in God's plan to save the world.

- What reward is available to those who suffer for doing good?

- How can someone lose (or keep) focus while sacrificing for something they believe in?

Read Romans 5:6-8. *"You see, at just the right time, when we were still powerless, Christ died for the ungodly. Very rarely will anyone die for a righteous person, though for a good person someone might possibly dare to die. But God demonstrates his own love for us in this: While we were still sinners, Christ died for us."*

- If Jesus is the example, how much are you willing to pay (or sacrifice) to truly follow in His steps?

Most of us will never be called upon to give our lives—our last breath—for the cause of Christ. But we're called by God to lay down our lives daily for His cause. It's a sacrifice of what we *could* have, what we *could* do, who we *could* be to follow God and allow Him to define those things. Many Christians choose *not* to make these sacrifices. Oftentimes, the choice isn't even a conscious one. It's simply that we live our lives with a facade of control, and we don't want to relinquish the dream that we have some measure of authority in our own lives, our own choices, our own decisions. But to *truly* follow Jesus, what we sacrifice is dominion over our own destiny. And *that* is a spiritual act of worship—laying aside our right to be in charge of ourselves and willfully handing that responsibility to God, regardless of the outcome.

3. GOD MAY ASK US TO SACRIFICE EVERYTHING FOR HIS PLAN.

Read Luke 9:23-25. *"Then he said to them all: 'Whoever wants to be my disciple must deny themselves and take up their cross daily and follow me. For whoever wants to save their life will lose it, but whoever loses their life for me will save it. What good is it for someone to gain the whole world, and yet lose or forfeit their very self?'"*

Read James 1:2-4. *"Consider it pure joy, my brothers and sisters, whenever you face trials of many kinds, because you know that the testing of your faith produces perseverance. Let perseverance finish its work so that you may be mature and complete, not lacking anything."*

Bobby sacrificed everything except his physical life. He gave up his career, his reputation, possibly his future. His faith was displayed in his action. He worshipped in sacrifice. He abdicated his will for the will of God. And he did it freely. He did it courageously. He did it because of his passion for God and compassion for people.

Sometimes when our sacrifice is painful, it's difficult to muster joy. But the truth is, James doesn't command us to find joy in the trial. He commands us to find joy in what the trial will eventually produce. That alone is another act of faith—believing in an unseen truth. Finding joy when sacrifice abounds is an act of worship, faith, and obedience.

- How much is too much sacrifice for your faith? How does sacrifice benefit us?

• What makes people hesitant to give up the world and its pleasures for God's plan?

The Bible is clear. Jesus makes plain statements to His followers about what He expects of His disciples. He is our sacrifice, and because of the benefit we receive in Christ, He intends for us to follow His example. The truth is, this world we live in no longer has anything to offer those of us who will eventually be going to live in God's kingdom. So, what do we really have to lose? We may suffer for Christ's sake, but God promises to be faithful in our sacrifice.

4. GOD IS FAITHFUL IN OUR SACRIFICE.

Read 1 Peter 4:19. *"So then, those who suffer according to God's will should commit themselves to their faithful Creator and continue to do good."*

• How should we deal with suffering in our lives?

• What does it look like for someone to "commit themselves to their faithful Creator"?

- Where do people who suffer and sacrifice for God find the strength to endure?

Read Hebrews 10:32-36. *"Remember those earlier days after you had received the light, when you endured in a great conflict full of suffering. Sometimes you were publicly exposed to insult and persecution; at other times you stood side by side with those who were so treated. You suffered along with those in prison and joyfully accepted the confiscation of your property, because you knew that you yourselves had better and lasting possessions. So do not throw away your confidence; it will be richly rewarded. You need to persevere so that when you have done the will of God, you will receive what he has promised."*

When sacrifice turns to suffering, it's hard to understand how someone could make the choice to willingly walk into hardship.

Imagine you own an old car that has brought you a lot of good memories. It is beat up, unreliable, and broken down, but it's yours and you love it. Now imagine that you have been given the opportunity to receive a brand-new vehicle, your dream car, if you enter a contest that requires you to stand in the sun and keep your hand on the vehicle for three days. Everyone who completes the task wins a new car. The one catch is that if you endure the task and win the car, you have to give up your old beloved car. Would you do it?

This is a very simplified illustration of the choice a person faces when asked to sacrifice for God's plan. The things that we have in this world are going to wear out, break down, and pass away whether we sacrifice or not. God has already prepared a place for us in heaven filled with unbelievable riches that will never rot. Sacrificing the sin-tainted things the world has to offer for the sake of doing good and following Christ's example offers a great reward. The choice is no contest for those who have faith.

Christians who understand the eternal reward that is to come will gladly sacrifice what the world has afforded them.

Read Matthew 5:11-12. *"Blessed are you when people insult you, persecute you and falsely say all kinds of evil against you because of me. Rejoice and be glad, because great is your reward in heaven, for in the same way they persecuted the prophets who were before you."*

- How does someone suffer to the point of joyfully accepting the sacrifices they are making to follow Jesus?

- What is promised to those who endure great sacrifice?

- How can you know that God will be faithful when you submit to His plan and it leads to sacrifice?

- Have you ever known someone who possessed joy during affliction? How is their story similar or different from your own?

Choosing to completely surrender to God's plan may mean great sacrifice. Our sacrifice may be misunderstood or go unnoticed by most of the world. One thing we can count on is that God will be faithful no matter what our circumstances. He promises a great reward to those who endure. He wants us to hold on to our confidence despite what the outcome of our suffering looks like.

Jesus sacrificed for our salvation, and He asks us to sacrifice for others. The sacrifice may cost us everything, but God promises to remain faithful to us always. Is Jesus worth your sacrifice?

Respond

- Take a personal inventory of your life:

    - What are some things you have already sacrificed for salvation?

    - What are you afraid God may ask you to sacrifice for His plan?

    - What is God currently asking you to surrender to Him?

– Are you willing to be used by Him no matter what the cost?

• Go to a quiet place, listen to some worship music, and think about what it means to be a living sacrifice. How are you fulfilling that description? How are you failing it? What is God asking you to do?

• Do you know anyone who is enduring hardship for God's plan? How can you encourage that person today? Make a plan to actively encourage that person as soon as possible.

PERSIST

Read Daniel 3:1-30 for encouragement.

Shadrach, Meshach, and Abednego were willing to face death in order to fully follow God's plan for their lives. Times had changed and with it new rules were enacted that contradicted their faith. These three friends stood strong even though it would have been easier to do what all the other people in their country were doing. It would have been understood and socially acceptable to keep their faith private, but they knew that was not what God wanted them to do. They risked everything, and God saved them.

CONCLUSION

From the beginning of creation, God has always had a plan to save the world from sin and despair. And since the beginning, we have been a part of that plan. God is at work all around us. Every moment is ordained. Every second is an opportunity. Every tick of the clock is an instant chance to act on what we believe. We fully participate in His plan by first choosing to embrace that relationship—that defining moment when we choose a relationship with Christ. And just as that moment was considered and planned on our behalf, God wants everyone to embrace that moment to know Him, trust Him, follow Him.

Participating in God's plan requires faith from the start—embracing what we cannot see to save us. Continuing that walk with Christ will also require faith. It will require taking a step with an unknown outcome. It will require trusting God enough to carry our cross into parts unknown. It will demand that we abandon logic at times. It will insist that we do something no one else would ever understand. But faith is useless without action. Without action, faith merely becomes knowledge. But the Bible clearly tells us in 1 Corinthians 13 that knowledge will eventually pass away. To fully love God—to trust Him with abandon—we must act when He shows us where He is at work. And the truth is, we want to! We want to scream His truth and compassion from the rooftops. But we're scared. We're unsure. We're timid. We're busy. We second-guess. We neglect.

But faith in action beckons us to sacrifice. We surrender caustic comforts that erode our resolve in order to proclaim our first love. Jesus asks us to deny everything the world offers and some of what we take for ourselves and follow His example of sacrifice. We may lose everything, but God is faithful. His generosity to His adopted sons and daughters is beyond all we could think or ask. Maybe we'll see that on this side of eternity. Or maybe our reward in heaven will be enough!

At the end of the day, rewards won't matter. And it won't matter that you watched this amazing movie, identified with the characters, or had an emotional moment. It won't amount to anything that you answered every question in this book or drew closer to your small group. What will matter is what you did with Jesus for those around you. What will matter is that faith moved beyond feeling for you. What matters is doing something.

So as you close this study guide, ask yourself the same question Malachi asked: "If you believe, then what are you gonna do about it?"